What
You
Should
Know
About the
Saints

What You Should Know About the Saints

Charlene Altemose, MSC

Liguori
One Liguori Drive
Liguori, MO 63057-9999
(314) 464-2500

Imprimi Potest:
Richard Thibodeau, C.SS.R.
Provincial, Denver Province
The Redemptorists

Imprimatur:
+ Paul A. Zipfel, V.G.
Auxiliary Bishop, Archdiocese of St. Louis

ISBN 0-7648-0047-7
Library of Congress Catalog Card Number: 96-78938

Cover design and interior art by Grady Gunter

Contents

Introduction

"Mommy, don't leave me alone in the dark," Amy sobbed as her mother tucked her in for the night.

"Remember, Amy, that God and your angel watch over you," Mother reassured her child.

"But I want somebody with skin on," the tot whimpered.

We smile at the child's naivete—yet we, too, react in the same way. We want to touch and feel that which we know. We simply relate better to "somebody with skin on."

God proved unconditional divine love, and sent "somebody with skin on" to live among us: Jesus. This is the essence of Christianity. "The Word became flesh and lived among us" (John 1:14): God sharing our humanity in Jesus. But we also see God's love in those who follow Jesus.

Suppose nobody took notice of Christ's suffering, death, and resurrection. There would be no Christianity today; no Church. But somebody did take notice: "those with skin on." And "those with skin on" kept alive the legacy of Christ's life and teachings. The

Church exists today primarily because these saintly men and women went forth into the world to spend themselves for Jesus in whom they believed and to whom they were totally committed. Persons came into the Church not because of its teachings, laws, and regulations, but because the ideals of Christ showed forth in flesh-and-blood human beings. The Church spread because "somebody with skin on" embodied Christian virtues.

In addition to our preference to relate to "somebody with skin on," we are drawn to those who seem larger than life. Something in our psyche attracts us to persons who possess the ideals we desire. The Halls of Fame, Hollywood's Sidewalk of the Stars, the Heisman trophy, Emmys, Tonys, Oscars: all these awards recognize those who excel in some way. These "heroes" help us grow to our full potential and are helpful in our life's challenges. In fact, so innate is this quest for identity with greatness that we often wish to establish a familiar rapport and intimacy with those we emulate. We are inspired to imitate those who are models for us.

These two human tendencies—our need for tangibles and our tendency to emulate greatness—provide the basic rationale for the Catholic practice of devotion to the Saints.

Saints are those people "with skin on" who, in their times, lived the Christian life to heroic degrees. From the earliest days, Saints have played a vital role in the development of the Catholic tradition. They stand apart as paragons of virtue because they followed Christ wholeheartedly.

This book looks at the role the Saints play in Catholics' devotional life and how the Saints have influenced the Church's development. We explore the role Saints play in our personal spirituality and, in keeping with the theology of the Second Vatican Council, the present-day understanding of what it means to be a Saint.

This book provides a general overview of the Church's teachings on the Saints. It clarifies misconceptions concerning Catholics' devotions to the Saints and answers questions such as "Why do Catholics pray to the Saints?" "What role do the Saints play in a Catholic's faith?" "How does the Church canonize a Saint?" "Do all Catholics pray to all the Saints?" "Why is devotion to the Saints an option?"

Part I explains the concept of "Saint" in two ways: in its broad sense and in its restricted meaning. The broad concept of "Saint" applies to each person's call to become a Saint. The restricted meaning applies to what we ordinarily understand "Saint" to mean: a holy person who, because of his or her heroic virtue and outstanding witness, has been officially recognized and canonized by the Catholic Church. Part I sets the groundwork; it distinguishes between these two meanings and discusses the traits that canonized Saints have in common.

Part II traces the history of the Church and the changes that the veneration of the Saints has undergone throughout the Church's two-thousand-year existence. It explains how the Saints have been proclaimed in the past and takes a look at the canonization process today.

Part III presents various ways Catholics honor the Saints in public worship and in personal prayer. It explains various customs that evolved and clarifies misunderstandings about Catholic piety and the Saints.

Part IV offers a potpourri of Saint trivia. It notes interesting facts gleaned from the lives of the Saints and highlights some of the perennial favorites.

If this work sparks in you an interest in the Saints and encourages you to read more about them, it has served its purpose. Your faith life, too, will be enriched, and you will be drawn closer to God and the spiritual life.

(For the sake of space, names of Saints will not be prefaced with the title "Saint" or the abbreviation "St." Also, this work does not explore Mary, the mother of Jesus. Because she is the quintessence of all holiness, Mary deserves a book of her own.)

PART I

Saints:
Broad and Restricted
Meanings

*A Saint is one who walks through
the dark paths of life, being a light in oneself.*

Anonymous

Once upon an eternity, God looked into the abyss and mused, "I am going to make me a world." So the Creator brought into existence a splendid, orderly array of galaxies, worlds, stars, and planets; even the divinity was dazzled. God smiled upon the magnificent universe but wasn't totally satisfied.

"Something is missing," God said. "Nothing in this creation can return my love and become my intimate friend." So, in divine wisdom, God chose a tiny and seemingly insignificant spot among the great galaxies. "I will bedeck this spot with all kinds of plants, trees, vegetation, and animals," God said. "I will make it a beautiful 'home' for a special creation, beings unlike any others in my creation. They will be of earth and of heaven, endowed with a natural life and a divine destiny. They will share my love, become my friends, and live with me forever."

God breathed a part of his own being into the ground of the earth—and man and woman stood before him, alive with the breath of the Divine, made in God's own image and likeness. "Now at last I have beings with whom I will share my life," God said, "who can enjoy this earth and become Saints."

This may sound like a paraphrase of the first chapter of Genesis. In reality, it's the ongoing story of a God who continues to love every human being. It is your story, my story, everyone's story.

Called by Name

With God, there is no past, present, or future. God had each of us in mind from all eternity. Just as our birth was characterized by a certain point in history, a specific place, and two special human beings as our parents, God gifts each of us with a unique love. "I have called you by name, you are mine" (Isaiah 43:1). God breathes the breath of life into us: "in the image of God he created them" (Genesis 1:27), gracing each of us with certain natural and supernatural gifts.

God not only knows the saintly potential in each of us, but gives us the necessary graces to accomplish this end. God has a unique image of us—what we can be—and no one in all creation can match that image. No one has our set of circumstances, our giftedness, our abilities, our opportunities. No one relates to God as we do. No one else can fill the divine plan God has especially for us. We exist to conform our lives to that image.

Our Response

But God respects our human dignity; God does not foist us into a relationship or force us into the divine mold. Rather, we are graced with the freedom to choose. We can decide whether or not we want a relationship with God.

This freedom doesn't happen easily, however. Because our human nature is tainted (theologically we call this "original sin"), we find it easier to live on a natural plane, attracted to that which draws us away from God. Even though we crave moral goodness and a life of virtue, we easily get caught up in the maelstrom of daily living and fail to make the best moral choices. We're so much like Paul, as he speaks of himself in his letter to the Romans: "I do not understand my own actions. For I do not do what I want, but I do the very thing I hate" (7:15).

Because we choose our own level of divine intimacy, we often fall short of the potential goodness God intends for us. We form a second, less idealistic image of ourselves: what we actually are.

For most of us, the two images that God has of us— what we *can be* in God's plan and what we actually *are*—are worlds apart. The task of bringing these two images closer together is a lifelong effort and requires heroic virtue. A wise saying on a banner summarizes the whole: "What you are is God's gift to you; what you become is your gift to God." *Sanctity Within Reach*

Fortunately, in God's divine providence and wisdom, sanctity is within our reach; we are well equipped for the journey. First, we have God's gift of "grace." This is not *something*, but *Someone*: God himself. Acting in and through us, God calls us to become Saints, and gifts us with sufficient grace to do so: "My grace is sufficient for you" (2 Corinthians 12:9). We also have the benefit of baptism, the visible expression of our desire to follow Christ. Through baptism, we are enabled to live on a spiritual level.

Needless to say, this is not a primrose path. The way to heaven is through the cross, as Jesus said: "Whoever does not take up the cross and follow me is not worthy of me" (Matthew 10:38). Yet, God gives us the necessary spiritual help to share the divine intimacy: the "state of grace."

Unfortunately, most of us are satisfied living our lives in an ordinary way. Day after day we go about our tasks, exerting only enough effort to do what is absolutely required and nothing more. We are content with the line of least resistance.

Canonization

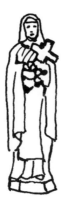

In the two-thousand-year history of the Church, millions of people have followed Christ in an ordinary, unheralded, and often unknown manner. Others have lived their Christian calling to an exceptional degree, demonstrating that the spiritual life is paramount. A comparatively small number of this latter group, about five thousand, are singled out and officially proclaimed "Saints" by the Catholic Church.

When we speak of the Saints, we ordinarily refer to those individuals who have been canonized—officially recognized as illustrating heroic spiritual virtues. Although other religions honor their holy ones in various ways, the Catholic Church is the only religious body that recognizes and honors its paragons of virtue with an official process. These paragons of virtue constitute the focus of this book.

When the Church canonizes a Saint, it infallibly declares that the person has led an exemplary life to a heroic degree, is in heaven, and is set up as a model of sanctity. Although the list, or canon, of Saints represents diverse personalities from each age of the Church, that which sets the Saints apart from ordinary persons is the outstanding virtue of their exemplary lives.

Common Characteristics of Saints

The Saints represent every age, nation, and spirituality in a diversity unmatched in other realms. If we look at the Saints collectively, however, common characteristics emerge. The analogy of "fitness," so epitomized in our culture, offers a clear framework for review of what sets the Saints apart. Just as we aspire to be "physically fit," and do all in our power to be so, the Saints are known to be "spiritually fit."

The Saints maintain balance by making wise choices. The Saints discern from God's viewpoint. They consciously blend God's image with the image they fashion in their own lives.

In making their life decisions, the Saints give special concern, first and foremost, to the good of the Church and the kingdom of God. Although they occasionally may not appear balanced according to worldly standards, the Saints are completely balanced in a spiritual sense. With feet planted firmly on mother earth, the Saints show us that heaven is our true home and that life here is the path we follow to arrive at our "true home." The Saints live on a two-dimensional level: in the world, yet not of the world. The spiritual world is as real to them as the earthly world.

The Saints align their lives to God's divine image of them. They struggle throughout life to fashion their image according to God's designs and are realistic in their outlook. They know their limits yet dare to take giant strides toward perfection.

The Saints are authentic. They do not put on airs or pretend to be what they are not. With the Saints, there is no pretense, no sham.

The Saints establish proper priorities: God first. While many "ordinary" people give God lip service and recognize God's existence, the Saints are on fire with the Divine. God flavors all their moments. Although fully human, the Saints are strangely familiar with God. As a result, they are as comfortable and intimate with the Lord as they are with their friends. In fact, the

Saints feel such an affinity with God that their own being fades where God's plans are concerned.

For the Saints, spirituality is not only an accessory of life; spirituality is the core and essence of their existence, giving substance to their whole purpose. The Saints incarnate a spiritual viewpoint into the mundane and natural in an exemplary manner.

A small child observing the stained glass windows in a church provides an apt definition of a Saint as "one through whom the light shines." The Saints are so attuned to the spiritual dimension of life that the light of God shines through them. They make Paul's words their own: "It is no longer I who live, but it is Christ who lives in me" (Galatians 2:20). The Saints truly are "other Christs" and not just ideals of God's goodness.

The Saints watch their spiritual diets. Just as we are a diet-conscious society, so too are the Saints, in another sense. Because they realize that life here on earth is only a journey toward their "real home"—eternity with God—the Saints are wary of imbibing too much of this world's comforts. They are careful not to become overweight with mundane concerns; they deny themselves many of the "good things" of life to maintain their spiritual well-being. The spiritual staples—the Word of God and the Eucharist—provide the Saints with strength and grace to work assiduously for God's kingdom on earth.

The Saints radiate spiritual well-being because their lives are flavored with the Divine. They do not suffer "virtue deficiency." Although the Saints mirror

holiness in varying degrees, their lives e
goodness and integrity that they nee
supplements."

The Saints recognize the importance of
the Saints are serious about the ad
cise. For them, exercise means keep
shape. They are not content with jogging the o
route; they are all marathoners in their own right.
They put in extra mileage, always doing more than is
required. The Saints heed Paul's admonition: "I do not
run aimlessly...but I punish my body and enslave it, so
that after proclaiming to others I myself should not be
disqualified" (1 Corinthians 9:26,27). The Saints tone
their spiritual muscles to be strong for the sake of
God's kingdom, and they scale the mountains of
heroic virtue and courage.

The Saints maintain a high level of energy. Because they
keep working at their spiritual fitness, the Saints can
make great strides in spreading the kingdom. They
have vision for what the Church needs at a certain
time in its history, and do not hesitate to roll up their
sleeves to get the work done, often despite overriding
odds. The Saints meticulously live the gospel challenge, to a valiant degree. They literally observe the
radical demands of Christ: "Be perfect...as your heavenly Father is perfect" (Matthew 5:48).

*The Saints work hard and constantly at maintaining their
spiritual fitness.* Although they are blessed with special
charisms and spiritual gifts, the Saints work hard to

"keep in shape." They live the axiom, "God provides for the birds of the air, but doesn't throw the food into their nests." They practice a nonsense approach to spirituality.

The Saints carry out their mission in life to a degree beyond the ordinary call to goodness. They work hard and seriously in responding to the radical demands of the Good News. They stumble; they sin; they fail. Yet, they begin over and commit themselves wholeheartedly to the graces of God working within. They are not Saints because they never fail; rather, they are Saints because they stumble, fall, struggle back to their feet, and try again. The Saints are "sinners who keep on trying."

For the Saints, there is no middle road; they live a one-hundred percent dedication and commitment. They sometimes go to extremes in living their vocation to holiness, practicing virtue to the point of senseless exaggeration, just to get the point across.

The Saints risk ridicule because of their fitness efforts. Because their personal standards and their worldly norms often clash, the Saints frequently are maligned. They dare to be "fools for the sake of Christ" (1 Corinthians 4:10) in unconditional commitment: "For to me, living is Christ and dying is gain" (Philippians 1:21).

Because of their countercultural approach to life, the Saints are sometimes misunderstood, and what they do is easily misinterpreted. The proverb "To live with saints in heaven is all honor and glory, but to live with saints on earth is quite another story" can apply to many holy persons.

"Sanctity doesn't necessarily consist in being odd, but sanctity does consist in being rare," Francis de Sales noted. The Saints truly are a rare breed of Christian.

The Saints manage stress by resting in the Lord. Because they know how to prioritize, the Saints seek refuge in intimacy with the Lord. Prayer and meditation bring them into close relationship with their God, who gives meaning to their lives. The Lord at times reveals divine love through mystical ecstasies.

The Saints dream great dreams for the sake of God's kingdom. They innovate and interpret the gospel message in new ways.

The Saints are not obsessed with spiritual progress. They wear their halos unobtrusively and camouflage their sanctity. In fact, the Saints do not know they are Saints because they do not strive to become known as such. A friend of Mother Cabrini remarked about her: "I knew her well and I didn't know she was a Saint—in fact, she didn't know that either."

The Saints, being gifted by God in extraordinary ways, use their gifts for the service of the kingdom of God, and not for their own glory.

The Saints master crisis-intervention techniques. They seem to be in the right place at the right time. The Church, often plagued with turmoil and confusion from both within and without, survived and continues to thrive because the Saints intervene with appropriate, often revolutionary solutions. When the Church is beset with strife, the fortitude of the Saints brings the Church through the difficulties and is instrumental in conflict resolutions. When the human element in the Church overshadows its divine mission, when the Church flounders in heresy and scandal, the Saints challenge authorities and come to the rescue.

Consider Leo the Great, who confronted Attila the Hun; recall Catherine of Siena, who challenged the pope to return to Rome from Avignon. Because of its fearless Saints, the Church endures through critical times.

The Saints have perfect vision. They tend to see more than the ordinary person sees. With their long-range vision, the Saints clearly see the needs of the Church and are not afraid to reach out and tackle the impossible. They see beneath the gruff exterior of the poor, the sores of the leper, the dullness of the ignorant, and the arrogance of power. Their eyes perceive new ways to interpret and live out the gospel. They truly see only with the heart. The Saints know that the genuine essentials of life are invisible to the eye.

The Saints have a keen sense of hearing and sturdy limbs. When it comes to spiritual wellness, the Saints do not need any hearing aids. They not only hear the wails of the oppressed, of the unlettered, of the troubled, but they listen intently to how the Lord is calling them to respond. Their auditory sense extends into their cardiac chamber, for they listen with their hearts as well as their ears—and they put into action what they hear.

The Saints stand firm and strong on all their principles and convictions. They never give in to convenience but bend only for justice and love. The Saints have no stiff joints, for they get their exercise by reaching out to others, especially those in need.

Despite their "fitness," however, the Saints suffer from numerous "maladies," according to human standards. But from God's viewpoint these "ills" are hallmarks of sanctity.

The Saints have enlarged hearts. As a result of extending tirelessly to those in need, the Saints' hearts possess an overwhelming capacity for love, empathy, and compassion. Their hearts are wide, encompassing those neglected by earthly standards.

The Saints have high "care pressure." They spend themselves tirelessly in the cause of every human cry. They "die to self" much sooner than their earthly flesh dies. They identify with the sufferings of others and bear their crosses with equanimity and courage. They put their lives on the line for others, with J-O-Y (Jesus - Others - You) as their motto.

The Saints are highly allergic (to evil and sin). Their crystalline integrity makes them ultrasensitive to the inconsistencies around them. The Saints are highly allergic to the evils and discrepancies of the day and courageously speak out against anything that does not portray goodness. Because of their disgust with evil and sin, the Saints suffer much. They see and experience the base standards rampant in the world, which leaves a painful imprint on their sensitive souls.

The Saints have a low tolerance for pain. They hurt and cry with others; their clarion call is "Your care in my heart." The Saints weep much—not for themselves, but for the pain and suffering of others. They are vulnerable and often in great pain because they deeply feel the miseries of the world.

The Saints have tired eyes that grow weary from their tears; they have hoarse voices from screaming out against the ills of society. They identify with those who suffer. When violence and inhumanity make headlines, the Saints offer hope and trust. Consider the heroic virtue of Father Damien, the leper priest, and Maximilian Kolbe, who gave up his own life in a Nazi concentration camp so that a father be spared for his family.

The Saints suffer from hardening of the "ought-eries." Because they perceive what *ought* to be done to further the kingdom of God, the Saints stop at nothing to accomplish the divine will. Once they realize they are called to a certain mission, they work with an insatiable passion and evangelistic drive to carry out their convictions.

Most of the Church's progress and many of the innovative movements within the Church are achieved because the Saints suffer this particular "malady." No human obstacle deters them, for they are firmly convinced that God calls them to a specific mission. Consider Joan of Arc, the French peasant girl who led the French army to victory.

Although we Catholics believe that we all come to God through Christ our mediator, we also believe that the Saints are effective channels for God's blessings to us. We believe that the Saints support us in our own quest for spiritual fitness, that they challenge us to go the extra mile, to be more than we are, to achieve our potential of goodness and perfection. We rely on the Saints to point us toward the correct path because we see that their own lives embody the ideals to which we are called. The Saints appeal to us because we relate our plights with theirs.

The lives of the Saints encourage us toward holiness more than a thousand sermons. Precepts do not convert; persons do. Lives, not lectures, provide models for sanctity. The Saints do just that. We consider the Saints as powerful advocates before God, helping in time of need and challenging us to greater heights of holiness.

The Saints generate divine power. They are the lifeblood of the Church. They energize the Church when it suffers, bringing calm and serenity in times of strife and turmoil. The prophetic voices of the Saints speak out against evils and proclaim new ways the gospel can be interpreted.

Conclusion

PART II

The Canonization Process

God creates out of nothing—
but he does far more.
God makes Saints out of sinners.

Sören Kierkegaard

I n each age of the Church, countless men and women lived the faith to a heroic degree. These people were the driving force behind the Church's rapid spread to all lands. With the title "Saint," the Church honors those who, graced with particular insights and visions, have acted on gospel values with radical commitment.

The way in which the Church has come to recognize the greatness of these noble souls evolved through the years. Likewise, the Church's definition of "sanctity" has changed. The following timeline profiles how this process has unfolded through history.

The Evolution of Recognizing Holiness

The Apostolic Age: The term "Saint" is derived from the Latin word *sancti*, which means "holy ones." The term was first used for a baptized follower of Christ. Paul exhorts the Church at Philippi to "Greet every saint in Christ Jesus" (Philippians 4:21), and he wrote "To the saints and faithful...in Colossae" (Colossians 1:2). Many of those who committed themselves wholly to Jesus died for the faith they professed. Later, the followers of Christ were called "Christians," and those who died in Christ were called "Saints."

A.D. *64-313 (Age of persecution):* During the persecutions under the Roman empire, many who professed their belief in Christ were slain for their faith. They were called "martyrs," from the Greek word *martyrion*, which means "witness." To sacrifice one's life for Christ was considered the ultimate proof of sanctity.

Honoring martyrs at their grave sites was a common practice of the early Christians. The anniversary of the

death was marked by a liturgy at the martyr's burial site or place of execution. It was believed that the prayers to God through the intercession of martyrs were especially powerful. Churches were built at the tombs of martyrs, and eventually relics of martyrs were embedded in the altar stones, a practice observed to this day.

When the persecutions ceased, the veneration of the martyrs continued and, in fact, increased in the third and fourth centuries. The events of the persecutions were retold and recorded and, like all oral tales, details were exaggerated and magnified. Through the years, as the stories of martyrs came to be embroidered with miraculous accounts, superstitions developed. Gradually, the relics and remains of martyrs came to be a way of keeping alive the memory of their heroic faith.

The veneration of Saints can be attributed to the grass-roots faith of the people; it is not a practice imposed by Church authorities.

A.D. 300-500 (*Age of confessors and ascetics*): Because the Edict of Milan (A.D. 313) allowed Christians to practice the faith openly, martyrdom "en masse" became a thing of the past. Ascetics became models of holiness because of their "living martyrdom" in personal practices of total detachment, fasting, and prayer. The faithful continued to honor holy persons, especially virgins, confessors who witnessed to the faith, and apologists who wrote in defense of the faith.

During this time, the cult of the Saints and martyrs spread rapidly. Chapels and churches were built at the tombs of the Saints, each town and village had its patron Saint, and lists of the holy ones of a locale were exchanged with other churches. Soon the lists or "canons" of Saints multiplied; a reputation for holiness and the bishop's approval were the basic criteria for sanctity.

A.D. 500-1000 (Early Middle Ages): Pope Gregory the Great (A.D. 590-604) stabilized the liturgy, initiated a liturgical calendar, and encouraged the cult of the Saints by including Saints' names in the eucharistic prayer and by celebrating their feast days. Devotion to the Saints further spread when missionaries took tales of these heroic people to the lands they converted.

But by now, the Church was in turmoil. Although local bishops permitted devotions in honor of those whose lives evidenced great virtue or miracles, holy persons were generally acclaimed by the populace. The cult of local Saints originated probably because favors were received on that person's behalf after he or she died. The reputation about the holy person's assistance spread.

Since oral storytelling was the basic means of communication, it's easy to see how accounts of these holy ones became embellished in the telling. You know what happens when a story is passed on by word of mouth; it's a "whispering-down-the-alley" effect. Legends handed on became somewhat distorted after generations of retelling.

A.D 1000-1200 (beginning of papal canonizations): After the Orthodox split in 1054, the bishop of Rome continued to wield influence in the Western Church.

Rome, the center of the Western Church, began setting standards in all aspects of Church life, including the affirmation of sainthood. The Church gradually realized, however, that abuses easily creep in when Saints are declared by popular acclaim. Thus, the pope began assuming power in this regard.

The first recorded canonization in a papal ceremony for the universal Church was the canonization of Ulric, bishop of Augsburg, in A.D. 993 by Pope John XV. By 1200 the right to canonize was reserved to the Holy See.

The Fourth Lateran Council in 1215, which initiated procedures for Church laws, included general norms for sainthood. These norms, however, were not rigidly enforced.

A.D. *1200-1500 (Middle Ages):* This was a time of instability for the Church. Because rituals were prayed in Latin—which the ordinary person could not understand—the laity felt alienated. As a result, they turned to other pious practices, namely devotion to the Saints. Although the papacy reserved the right to canonize officially, the people acclaimed their own Saints.

This was also a time when devotion to the human aspect of Christ became common: the crèche at Christmas, for example, and the Stations of the Cross commemorating our Lord's passion. Understandably, the cult of Mary and the Saints grew along with devotion to the humanity of Christ. The details of the lives of the Saints gained the same popularity that today's tabloids enjoy. The people knew their Saints better than they knew Scripture.

During this time, popular devotions escalated and pilgrimage sites multiplied. Each town and village honored a special Saint, and the feast day was often a civic festival—a custom that prevails in some ethnic neighborhoods in the United States. Although excesses and exaggerations were discouraged by Church leaders, the people's choice often prevailed and Saints' devotions flourished.

Those Saints known for their power of intercession in specific cases were readily set up as "patrons" of particular human needs. Thus the list of patron Saints for each cause has grown and is still extant today.

Canonizations continued, but many of the Saints who died in the twelfth and thirteenth centuries were canonized shortly after their deaths, with no investigation or distinction made between beatification and canonization.

1500-1600 (the Reformation and the Council of Trent): The Protestant reformers rejected the Saints as intermediaries before God; they believed that Christ alone was the sole mediator. The Saints, they reasoned, detracted from Christ's role. At times the reformers' violent reactions led to the destruction of images, statues, and works of art.

The Council of Trent (1545-1563), however, upheld the Catholic practice of devotion to the Saints and enforced standard canonization norms. In 1588 Pope Sixtus V set up the Sacred Congregation for Rites to study the lives of holy persons recommended for canonization.

In 1634 Pope Urban VIII set forth guidelines for the

process of canonization, with beatification as a separate step. Canonizations continued as well as pious practices and legends about the Saints.

1600-1960: Around 1630 a group of Belgian Jesuit scholars, under the direction of John Bolland, undertook the tedious task of sifting through the lives of the Saints to separate legendary elements from historical data. The resulting volumes, *Acta Sanctorum*, document the Saints' lives with accuracy, free from legends. The Bollandists' research has been an asset to the Church and continues to this day.

In 1738 Pope Benedict XIV discussed canonization in a treatise titled "Of Beatified Servants of God and Canonization of Saints." These norms were adapted by the 1917 Code of Canon Law and were observed until 1983, when "New Laws for the Causes of Saints" was published in Rome.

The Second Vatican Council: In its renewal of all areas of the Church, the Second Vatican Council (1962-1965) desired to restore balance in spirituality and thus make the Church more meaningful for modern times. To focus on Christ as the center of liturgy, obvious radical changes took place, which especially affected Catholic piety and devotion to the Saints.

The altar of sacrifice became the focal point, for example, and images or statues of Saints were relegated to less dominant positions. Naturally, Catholics who had particular devotions to the Saints became upset when statues were removed or placed in less conspicuous places in their churches. Although Vatican II did not totally ban statues of Saints in churches, it did caution that "they should be restricted in number and their relative positions should reflect right order" (Constitution on the Sacred Liturgy, #125). It further instructed that the faithful put devotions to the Saints in proper perspective and maintain a balance: "The authentic cult of the saints does not consist so much in a multiplicity of external acts, but rather in a more intense practice of our love....Our relationship with the saints in heaven...in no way diminishes the worship of adoration given to God the Father, through Christ, in the Spirit; on the contrary, it greatly enriches it" (Dogmatic Constitution on the Church, #51).

Revision of the Roman Calendar

A major reform brought about by Vatican II was the revision of the Roman calendar of Saints by Pope Paul VI in 1969.

The apostolic letter, *The Celebration of the Paschal Mystery*, sets forth definite principles concerning veneration of the Saints:

- The history and lives of the Saints in the liturgical calendar were critically analyzed.
- The number of devotional feasts was lessened.
- Many Saints' feasts were dropped from liturgical observances. (Only those Saints of universal significance appear in the general Church calendar, and these represent every period of time and every race.)

Because historical data was lacking on some of the Saints, the Church suppressed certain liturgical feasts.

Contrary to opinion, the Church did not "de-canonize" these Saints or "get rid of them"; it simply removed their feast days from liturgical observance. Popular private prayers and devotions to these Saints, however, may and do continue.

The Congregation for the Causes of Saints

In 1969, Pope Paul VI divided the Congregation of Rites into the Congregation for Divine Worship and the Congregation for the Causes of Saints. Besides overseeing all causes introduced for sainthood, the Congregation for the Causes of Saints is responsible for the preservation of relics and conferral of the title "Doctor." It exercised this latter prerogative in 1970, when Catherine of Siena and Teresa of Avila were the first women to be named Doctors of the Church.

The Cult of the Saints and the Revised Canon Law

Book IV of the Code of Canon Law (canons 1186-1190), revised in 1983, deals with the cult of the Saints, sacred images, and relics. It upholds and promotes the Church's devotion to the Saints, but allows public veneration only to those who have been beatified or canonized. Canon 1403 rules that canonization cases are governed by special pontifical law.

The new Code of Canon Law also revised the question of names given at baptism. The Council of Trent decreed that the baptismal name be that of a Saint; if the name chosen was not that of a Saint, a Saint's name was usually substituted. Today, although the custom of naming a child after a Saint is still encouraged, the revised Code of Canon Law (canon 855) states that the name given in baptism "be not alien to Christian sentiments."

Although Pope John Paul II issued new norms for the making of Saints (*The Teaching of Divine Perfection*, 1983), canonization proceedings are still complex. The latest norms stress the use of scientific and historical evidence coupled with a spiritual discernment process in the investigation of causes for sainthood. The Congregation for the Causes of Saints, the Vatican's administrative body responsible for beatification and canonization, meticulously scrutinizes each case.

Steps in the Canonization Process

To be declared a Saint, one must have displayed obvious, personal, heroic virtue. Yet, the canonization process proceeds only if public acclaim, diplomatic pressure, and adequate funds are also available. Although the steps through the process can be long, they are clear.

Initiating the cause for sainthood: The road to sainthood begins with the local bishop in whose diocese the person resided. The bishop must provide adequate proof of heroic virtue and reputation for sanctity on the local level. A postulator appointed by the bishop is responsible for compiling all the documents of the case. Details of the person's life, witness accounts by those who knew the person, and all writings and communications by the person are presented to the Congregation for the Causes of Saints in Rome. The Congregation then meticulously analyzes and determines whether all is in order.

Because the expenses incurred in this process can be major, "sponsors" support and contribute monies to the cause to keep it moving. Most Saints who have been canonized since the process of canonization was standardized have been members of religious communities or prominent in the Church. This is not surprising when we consider the fact that the process is complex and expensive, and that many persons must be interested enough in the project, with sufficient commitment and funds to carry the process through to canonization.

Acceptance of the cause ("venerable"): When Rome accepts and approves the documents regarding the one recommended for sainthood, the person is considered "venerable," and private devotion is allowed. Usually the person's cause continues toward beatification. Sometimes, however, the cause is stymied, and the person remains "venerable," possibly because no authentic miracle required for beatification is forthcoming, or for some other legitimate cause.

"Blessed": The Congregation for the Causes of Saints intensely scrutinizes the life, virtues, reputation for holiness, ministry, and writings of the person. One miracle is required to be named "blessed." This is usually a physical healing that can be definitively and scientifically proven, indicating that natural laws have been lifted through the intercessions of the one considered for sainthood. Persons who die as martyrs are exempt from the miracle requirement.

When an authentic miracle—due to the intercessory power of the "venerable"—is "proved," and after approval by the Sacred Congregation, the matter is presented to the pope. If the pope judges the person's holiness as exemplary, the person is declared "blessed." This process is called "beatification."

The beatification ceremony includes a papal declaration of the person's holiness, a solemn Mass, and a prayer to the "blessed." The person can be honored with a specific Mass and prayers in the Liturgy of the Hours only in one's diocese, country, or religious community. The person is not enrolled in the official calendar of the universal Church until canonization.

Beatification is no longer a separate process but a preliminary step toward sainthood, because canonization is the ultimate goal. Until recent times, the beatification ceremony took place in Rome. Since Pope John Paul II travels extensively, he has used the opportunity to beatify in other places. For example, Blessed Peter Torot, a lay catechist of Papua, New Guinea, slain for his faith in 1945, was beatified in June, 1994 when the pope visited the South Seas.

Notable "blesseds" from the United States include Mother Katherine Drexel, foundress of the Sisters of the Blessed Sacrament; Kateri Tekakwitha, "Lily of the Mohawks" and convert to Christianity; and Father Junipero Serra, pioneer in the California missions.

"Equivalent beatification or canonization": The pope can decide to omit some procedures—requirement of a miracle or further investigation into one's life, for example—through "equivalent beatification or canonization." This is usually determined by the person's established reputation, as was the case of Fra Angelico, the Renaissance artist whom Pope John Paul II beatified in 1983.

Canonization: After beatification, investigations continue, although causes may be delayed for long periods of time. (Presently there are many cases "in deferral," the time between the introduction of the cause and actual canonization.) To advance the person's cause to sainthood, a second miracle is usually required at this point.

The canonization of a Saint is infallibly pronounced by the pope in a formal declaration called an "apostolic bull," and the canonization ceremony is usually celebrated amid the pageantry of Saint Peter's in Rome. The pope declares that the person is in heaven, is worthy of public veneration, and is included in the liturgical calendar of the universal Church. The official pronouncement of a Saint:

- allows public honor and veneration of the Saint
- permits churches to bear the Saint's name
- allows for a liturgical feast to be placed on the universal calendar of the Church
- permits images of the Saint to be publicly displayed
- allows the Saint's relics to be publicly honored

Official Church Teaching

The *Catechism of the Catholic Church,* issued in 1993, states Church teachings on the Saints. The numbers at the end of each summary statement below denote the corresponding paragraph numbers in the *Catechism.*

The work of salvation and the outpouring of the Spirit continue to be manifested through the witness of the Saints (686, 688).

The Church honors the Saints who are in heaven, officially recognizes them by canonization, holds them up as models, and encourages the faithful to pray to them so they may intercede to God on behalf of the faithful (956, 957, 962).

Throughout each age in the Church, persons outstanding in holiness have been recognized as models for our imitation. The canonization process recognizes the continuing power of the Holy Spirit at work in the Church (828).

All the faithful are bonded together in a spiritual unity and share in the spiritual goods of the Church through the Communion of Saints. Those who are closely united to Christ—the Saints in heaven—intercede for the faithful on earth (946-959).

We discover the holiness in the Church in the long history of its Saints, and we celebrate the Saints in the sanctoral cycle of the liturgical year (2030).

Images of the Saints honor the memory of those they portray and lead one to God, who alone is adored and worshipped (2131, 2132).

The name of a Saint can be given in baptism as a model of one to emulate (2156).

Conclusion

The vitality and productivity of the Church has been accomplished chiefly by the works and deeds of the holy men and women who worked tirelessly for the spread of God's kingdom. Each age, blessed with dedicated Saints, has endured through many crises because of these holy ones.

Canonization is the Church's means of recognizing its great ones in a solemn way. In comparison to the many who deserve the honors, canonization continues to be a rare and exceptional event. It is reserved to only a few, compared to the great number of persons who have followed Christ most perfectly and have demonstrated exemplary virtue.

Because canonization is a complex and lengthy process, many persons who rightly deserve to be canonized remain anonymous, known only to God. In fact, we may have some pleasant surprises when we get to heaven and find that those we least expected to be revered actually enjoy the same intimacy with God as those we esteemed by our earthly standards.

PART III

Devotion to and Veneration of the Saints

*The Saint is not so because one is primarily good;
but one is a Saint because one is transparent
for something other than self.*

Anonymous

D evotion to the Saints is rooted in a belief in the Communion of Saints, which we Catholics affirm each time we pray the Creed. We believe that we are linked in a close-knit spiritual relationship, bonded in the grace and love of God. The Saints, the souls in purgatory, and we pilgrims on earth "form one body, the good of each is communicated to the others" (*Catechism of the Catholic Church*, 947). Those in heaven assist us here on earth, and we on earth pray for those in purgatory.

The Saints provide a sense of contact and fellowship with us by maintaining an interest in worldly affairs. When we pray to the Saints we ask them to pray to God for us. In life, too, we often use intermediaries to plead on our behalf. When we were children, we may have asked Mom to ask Dad for something we wanted. "You ask for me" is a common ploy we use when we want others to solicit favors for us. So also we ask the Saints to help us.

Contrary to popular opinion, however, Catholics do not worship the Saints—although exaggerated piety gives that impression at times. The tribute we render to the Saints differs from our adoration of God. Nonetheless, as models of virtue, the Saints are worthy of honor and imitation.

In English there are no specific words to make the distinction between divine worship and veneration of the Saints. Thus, we use Latin terms. *Latria* is the adoration we pay to God and Jesus alone. Honor paid to the Saints and the angels is of a different kind and degree, called *dulia*, which can be translated as "fitting and appropriate respect."

Why Catholics Pray to the Saints

45

When a person is canonized a Saint, the Church proclaims that the person can be publicly honored. Over the years the Church has venerated Saints in liturgy and official commemorations.

Eucharistic Prayers: From the time of Gregory the Great, names of Saints were included in the Eucharistic Prayer (Canon of the Mass). The renewed liturgy of Vatican II provides four options of the Eucharistic Prayer, in which the Saints' intercessions are invoked.

The first Eucharistic Prayer retains the ancient listing of Saints: "In union with the whole Church, we honor...." The list includes many martyrs and Saints of the early Church. In the second Eucharistic Prayer we pray that "the Saints who have done your will throughout the ages make us worthy to share eternal life." In the third option we pray that "we may be enabled to share in the inheritance of the Saints, especially..." and the names of Saints can be inserted. In the fourth option we pray, "Grant to us to enter our heavenly inheritance in the company of Mary, the apostles and the Saints."

Advent

Christmas

Lent

Easter

Pentecost

ORDINARY
TIME

The liturgical calendar: The liturgical calendar is planned in a way that celebrates the mysteries of Christ each year in cycles and seasons: Advent, Christmas, Lent, Easter, Pentecost, and Ordinary Time. Gradually there evolved, concurrent with the liturgical seasons, another cycle of feasts in honor of the Saints, the "sanctoral cycle." In time this calendar became cluttered with so many Saints that the significance of the mysteries of salvation of the liturgical seasons was overshadowed. Thus, in the revised Roman calendar of 1969, the number of Saints' feasts has been drastically lessened so that feasts commemorating the mysteries of salvation take precedence. According to their importance for the universal Church, feasts of Saints are observed as solemnities, feasts, or obligatory memorials.

Besides those in honor of Christ and Mary, the Saints' solemnities are: Joseph, foster father of Jesus, March 19; the birth of John the Baptist, June 24; Apostles, Peter and Paul, June 29; and All Saints, November 1. In many countries these are holy days; the United States observes only the Solemnity of All Saints, November 1, as one of its six holy days of obligation.

Saints whose liturgical remembrances are classed as "feasts" include the apostles, the evangelists, and the martyrs (Paul, Stephen, Lawrence, and the Holy Innocents). The Feast of the Archangels, celebrated on September 29, is also observed as a "feast."

Saints considered important for the universal Church are remembered in obligatory memorials which must be commemorated if no other feast supersedes. The obligatory memorials in the 1969 revised Roman calendar reflect the universal and multicultural character of the Church. Some of the Saints in the sixty-nine obligatory memorials (according to the Sacramentary) observed in the United States include Agnes, Agatha, Paul Miki and companions, Polycarp, Philip Neri, Justin, Boniface, Mary Magdalen, Mother Cabrini, John Neumann, and Peter Claver.

Saints who are significant for a particular country,

church, or religious community are remembered with liturgical observance in optional memorials. When there is no other feast superseding, the priest can choose to celebrate liturgy in honor of the Saint.

Liturgy of the Hours: The Saints are also commemorated in the public liturgical daily prayer of the Church: the Liturgy of the Hours. Each day is sanctified, and the Church is unified by the collective prayers of clergy, religious, and laity who join with the Saints in intercession to God for the good of the whole Church.

Personal Piety and Devotion to the Saints

We also relate to and communicate with the spiritual world in subjective personal terms. This spirituality is expressed in a variety of ways and evolves as does our personality and growth. Each of us fashions a unique spirituality by which we come to God on our own "faith wavelength." Catholics have a vast array of ways in which we express our personal faith; the cult of the Saints is one such means. The most common ways we reverence and respect the Saints are through various prayer forms and by visual representations.

We use the word "cult" to define our personal piety and devotion to the Saints and the ways this relationship is expressed in pious practices. This is in contrast to the derogatory sense with which the word "cult" is usually associated.

Prayers: As humans, we are great "pray-ers." When we feel helpless in life's mysteries and problems, our human nature naturally turns to prayer as a source of power and strength.

One of the most common ways Catholics pray to the Saints is in intercessory prayer, by which we ask the Saints to intercede for us to God for a special favor.

We believe that God hears our prayers through the intercession of the Saints, and so we ask the Saints to pray to God on our behalf. We unite with the Saints in prayer to God; the Saints have "pull" with God, but no divine power in themselves.

Prayers to the Saints can either be spontaneous or set formulas composed by someone else, as those on prayer cards or in prayer books. Prayers to Saints conclude with "through Christ our Lord" because answers to our prayers come to us through the redemptive merits of Jesus, who mediates God's graces and blessings.

Litanies: A litany is a series of short invocations prayed by a leader, the assembly responding with a brief rejoinder such as "pray for us." The Litany of the Saints, the oldest and most popular of litanies, is prayed during the Forty Hours devotion, Easter Vigil, ordinations, and religious profession ceremonies. A shortened form may be prayed at baptisms and confirmations. Other litanies approved for public use are the litanies of Loretto (Mary), the Sacred Heart, the Holy Name, the Precious Blood, and Saint Joseph. All other litanies are only for private prayer.

Novenas: In a pressing need, Catholics may turn to the devotion of a "novena," prayers said aloud with others or in private nine consecutive times. No set formula is required, but one invokes the aid of a particular Saint who is known to help in certain cases or for a special intention. Public novenas sometimes are held before a Saint's feast day. The novena tradition dates back to the apostles, who waited nine days in prayer for the coming of the Holy Spirit.

Beads: From earliest days, and even in other religions, persons have used beads to help focus attention to prayer. The rosary is the most commonly used form of beads in the Catholic Church, but other devotions have developed with the use of beads to aid one in meditating on the virtues of a particular Saint.

Votive candles: Light and fire have always symbolized a sacred presence. Many Catholic churches continue the tradition of vigil lights or votive candles. Representing prayers for blessings or favors, wax candles or electric bulbs burn before a statue or image of the Saint. Devotees light the candles or electric lights and offer a small donation as a prayerful act of devotion. Prayers are directed for a special intention, and one's presence continues as the light burns.

Art representations: Sacred art, born of artists' inspiration and vision, has well preserved the legacy handed on from the Saints. Just as we keep photos as cherished memories of our loved ones, from earliest times Catholics have used statues, medals, and pictures as reminders of the Saints and as aids in devotion. Images are given honorary places, adorned with flowers, have vigil lights burn before them, and often are kissed with reverence. Blessings attached to these objects set them apart as "sacred."

The Saints have provided inspiration for some of the greatest art in the Western world, expressed in all forms and mediums: mosaics, frescoes, murals, statues, canvasses, stained glass windows, illuminated manuscripts, engravings, and so forth.

Earliest Christian art was symbolized in cryptic form rather than images. But as relics of martyrs became less available, images became a viable substitute.

There was a time, of course, when all images were considered idolatrous, an idea that stemmed from Jewish and Islamic beliefs which taught that God could not be represented in any form. The Second Council of Nicaea in 787, however, rejected this notion, known as iconoclasm, and upheld the use of images in churches. To this day, the Eastern Christian churches refrain from the use of three-dimensional statues and represent the sacred on flat two-dimensional surfaces.

In ages when photography was nonexistent, artists grappled with ideas of how to depict the Saints. They attempted to portray the Saint's spirituality so that the Saint could be easily identified. Thus, they developed and employed emblems and symbols that clearly indicated what the Saint represented, often with the native place of the Saint as a backdrop.

Emblems, garb, or attire, for example, enables us to identify and convey the inner meaning of the virtue for which the Saint is known. The Saints often hold a symbol, such as a church or monastery, palms, swords, pens, quills, books, food, flowers, or instruments of torture, by which they can be recognized

Beginning in the fifth century, artists used the halo to indicate the holy status of a person. This was an idea borrowed from the Greeks and Romans who used the halo to show close association with the gods. A halo is distinguished from the aureole, an aura of light that encircles one's whole body, as depicted in resurrection scenes or in scenes depicting visions of Mary.

Keep in mind that artistic representations *remind* us of the Saint: they are not objects of veneration in themselves. Neither do Catholics *pray to* the statues or images of Saints. These are mere visual aids to help us relate to the Saints.

Also keep in mind that the Church protects its precious heritage of art by requiring permission of the local bishop for repairs on classic art pieces. The presence of sacred images in churches must be moderate in number and not detract from one's devotion.

Icons: Icons play a major role in the faith of Eastern Rite Catholics. These two-dimensional images are not looked upon as mere art forms, but represent the divine presence in the world. The artistic icon style—elongated faces, bold piercing eyes, and large hands—symbolizes the spiritual which reaches beyond time.

Each icon upholds a long tradition and is the copy of another icon that already exists. Painting icons is a sacred calling and ministry. Icons usually portray Christ, Mary, the apostles, and evangelists.

Relics: From early days, Mass was celebrated over the tombs of Saints. Their body parts, personal belongings, or soil from their grave sites came to be coveted as "sacred" and revered as relics because these were intimately connected with the Saint.

The popularity of relics reached its height during the Crusades and the Middle Ages. Honors and reverence given to the relics were as grandiose as if the Saint were present in person. Relics often were displayed in ornate receptacles, called reliquaries, and people vied for their precious possession. Naturally, this penchant led to abuses and superstitions connected with relics. People used them as charms and amulets, hoping they would bring good luck and fortune. Used devotionally, however, relics and all sacred objects can act as conduits of grace and God's blessings. Relics inspire us and put us into greater contact with the "holy."

Relics are categorized in three classes. First class relics are part of the body of the Saint. Second class relics are objects used or clothing worn by the Saint. Third class relics, the most common and available, are objects that have been touched to a first or a second class relic.

The Church decrees that fixed altars contain a relic of a martyr, and it forbids the selling of relics.

Medals: The use of medals originates from the practice of ancient civilizations that imprinted images of their rulers on coins. Medals are used and worn by Catholics so that the memory and spiritual blessings of a particular Saint are always present.

Scapulars: The scapular is a long sleeveless garment draped over the shoulders as part of the monastic religious habit. So that the laity could share in the

monastic spiritual blessings, personal scapulars were developed: small rectangular pieces of cloth connected by ribbon and worn around the neck, front and back. Scapulars carry with them indulgences and blessings for the wearer. Most scapulars are in honor of Jesus or Mary.

Shrines: When that which is holy touches a place, the aura often remains long afterward. Places connected with the sacred have become places of respect, reverence, and pilgrimage. Chaucer's *The Canterbury Tales* evolved from a pilgrimage to Thomas Becket's grave site. Today, places where Saints ministered are often turned into devout pilgrimage sites.

The mystique of a "holy place" was made real for me several years ago as we traveled through miles of barren strip mines that dominate the countryside near Hecksherville in northeastern Pennsylvania. I was assured by my guide that there really was a beautiful church in the midst of this seeming wasteland.

This place is special because Bishop John Neumann, C.SS.R., the first American male Saint, established a parish here. As we rounded the bend in the road, Saint Kieran's Church stood majestic in contrast to the bleak surroundings. Built by hardworking miners who carried the stone from the mountain, the church in progress was seen by Bishop Neumann himself. Inside the church, a mural depicts the life of this saintly bishop; the confirmation record in the Saint's handwriting rests on a prie-dieu.

As I knelt and placed my hands reverently on the book, I felt a mystical bond with this humble, great man of God. "Surely the presence of the Lord is in this place," I prayed. Since that day my devotion to this saintly bishop has grown, as has my conviction that a holy presence continues in the aura of sacred places.

Hagiography: Scan the bestseller lists or browse the biography section of a bookstore. Consider the human penchant for TV soap operas. Obviously, we like stories about people. People's lives fascinate and interest us.

Our ancestors in the faith believed that Christ's message and example were kept alive in the simple stories of holy people. Through storytelling, the heritage and legacy of the Saints have been passed on. However, through the transmission of stories by word of mouth, their wonders and virtues have been embellished at times.

Since the early days of the Church, biographers of the Saints, called "hagiographers," documented the details of Saints' lives. What's more, many Saints have left accurate records of their lives through their memoirs and autobiographies.

These written accounts are preserved in various forms: liturgical texts, calendars, biographies, and legends. Though the lives of the Saints are filled with miracles and incredible legends, they form a rich reference of the customs and the lifestyles of peoples in a specific age of the Church.

Collections of the résumés of Saints' lives have been a popular source of general information about the Saints. A perennial favorite of these collections is Butler's *Lives of the Saints.*

The lives of the Saints are also made known through

other media. Videos, documentaries, and comic books portray the Saints graphically in our communications-conscious age. These are especially popular in the religious education of our young people.

Two famous award-winning films based on Saints' stories are *Song of Bernadette*, which is the account of Mary's appearances to Bernadette Soubirous at Lourdes, France, and *A Man for All Seasons*, which is the account of Thomas More, who was executed because he refused to accept Henry VIII as head of the Church of England.

In addition to the accounts that others have collected about the Saints, we have the firsthand writings of many Saints. While many of these writings have been lost in time, others have endured and are perennial spiritual classics. These works help us to grow in the spiritual life and explain the mysteries of faith. Some of these classics include *Introduction to a Devout Life* by Francis de Sales; *Spiritual Exercises* by Ignatius of Loyola; *The Dark Night of the Soul* by John of the Cross; *The Interior Castle* by Teresa of Avila; *Story of a Soul* by Thérèse of Lisieux, the Little Flower; *Confessions* and *City of God* by Augustine; *Summa Theologica* by Thomas Aquinas; and *Moral Theology* by Alphonsus Liguori.

Folklore: Pious practices evolve from folklore and do not carry ecclesial sanction because they often resemble superstition. If one performs such an act with faith and dependence on God, however, there is no harm. But these practices ordinarily evolve into superstitious acts. Some believe, for example, that if they place a statue of Saint Joseph upside down in the ground, they will sell their house. Some people put statues on the window sill if they want "good" weather—whatever that may mean to them at the time. The practice of putting a medal or statue of Saint Christopher on the car dashboard for protection is a common pious devotion even by those who are not Catholic.

Although the Saints assist us in our needs, we may succumb to the temptation to use their help as ploys and manipulations. In our devotions and prayers we cannot attempt to control the supernatural. We need to remember that we are limited and depend on a greater Power: God. Our prayers and devotions must reflect this attitude of faith and acceptance of God's will. A medal, for example, is to be worn in faith and not used as a charm or amulet. There have been cases reported, however, of persons saved from death because a medal was worn, especially of a soldier in battle.

When reading legends and tales of remarkable, unbelievable events in the lives of the Saints, remember that the Saints received special spiritual gifts. While God can and does work miracles, even in our present age, we must not interpret these events as doctrines of faith. Private revelations are just that—private. While the message may inspire and move us toward a deeper faith, the Church exercises caution about visions and mystical experiences. It does not dictate that we believe in them.

We cannot consider our brief discussion of superstition and manipulation complete without mention of chain letters and prayer guarantees. Pure and simple, chain letters requesting us to say a special prayer and pass it on to a certain number of people with the warning not to "break the chain" are superstitious. Chain letters should be torn up and thrown away. In the same vein, a prayer in the church pew, with the guarantee that if we say the prayer a certain number of times our favor will be answered, is manipulative and is not sanctioned as a Catholic practice.

Conclusion

Devotions to the Saints can enrich our relationship with God. Prayers, pious practices, pictures, and statues can inspire us toward a deeper spirituality and help us to focus our attention. In ages when reading was an elitist privilege, images as tools of learning have been called the "textbooks of the illiterate." The lives of the Saints encourage us in our life's challenges.

It is impossible for all Catholics to know the vast number of Saints, so we choose the ones to whom we pray. As our spirituality develops, so does our style of praying and choice of devotions. We are no less Catholic, however, if we do not "buy into" devotion to the Saints. Pious practices regarding the Saints is optional and secondary to our faith. But devotion to the Saints, if kept in proper perspective, is a valuable asset and guide in our quest for holiness.

PART IV

Saintly Potpourri

Saints are like the light of the stars, which still reaches the earth long after being extinguished. Saints touch us by radiating the light of Christ to us through their life and deeds.

Anonymous

Throughout history, Catholics have shown special devotion and reverence for certain Saints. No one person can know about all the Saints, of course, or have devotion to all of them. Catholics usually number a choice few among their advocates. We are either attracted to the life of the person and relate to it, or we pray to a particular Saint because of favors received.

Since we can pick and choose the Saints to whom we pray, I conducted an impromptu survey of several hundred people from different walks of life. I asked them to name five of their favorite saints, not including Mary, the Mother of Jesus. I found many of the popular and traditional favorites were named, but I also discovered that certain unknown Saints ranked high as favorites. As you scan the list, how many are you familiar with? Which Saints would you like to learn more about?

The five most popular Saints (and the causes for which they are noted) included Thérèse of Lisieux, the Little Flower (patron of missions); Joseph, foster father of Jesus (patron of carpenters and persons who are dying); Anthony of Padua (patron of those looking for lost items); Francis of Assisi (patron of ecologists and lovers of animals); and Teresa of Avila, a mystic (patron of those who suffer headaches).

The following list summarizes the rest of my survey results. The first group of Saints listed received the most—and the same—number of "votes." The second group received the second most—and the same—number of votes, and so forth.

Paul, apostle to the Gentiles (patron of persons who are in public relations)

Anne, the mother of Mary (patroness of housewives and women in labor)

Peter, apostle, first pope (patron of anglers)

Jude Thaddeus, apostle (patron of those caught in impossible and hopeless situations)

Catherine of Siena (patroness of those who work in nursing services; also a protector against fire)

Margaret Mary Alacoque (patroness of those with a special devotion to the Sacred Heart)

Michael the Archangel (patron of paratroopers, mariners, and grocers)

Gertrude, mystic (patroness of those with a special devotion to the Sacred Heart)

Ignatius of Loyola, founder of the Jesuits (patron of soldiers and of those on retreat)

Francis Xavier (patron of those who work in the missions, especially in India and Japan)

Patrick, apostle to Ireland (patron of anyone who has been bitten by a snake)

John Neumann, C.SS.R., founder of parishes (patron of those who pray Forty Hours devotions)

Rose of Lima, Peruvian Saint (patroness of the Americas)

John the Evangelist, author of the fourth gospel (patron of writers)

John of the Cross, mystic (patron of spiritual directors)

Bernadette Soubirous (patroness of those with a devotion to Our Lady of Lourdes)

Christopher (patron of travelers, motorists, sailors, and porters)

Lucy (patroness of those who suffer eye diseases)

Joan of Arc (patroness of the French and of soldiers)

Maria Goretti, martyr (patroness of victims of rape)

John the Baptist, forerunner of Jesus (patron of blacksmiths)

Margaret of Scotland (patroness of queens, widows, and large families)

Stephen, first martyr (patron of deacons)

Elizabeth of Hungary (patroness of bakers, widows, people who are falsely accused, and people who are homeless)

Blessed Kateri Tekakwitha (patroness of North American Indians)

John Bosco, founder of the Salesians (patron of editors and those who work for, live in, or support schools for orphan boys)

Elizabeth, cousin of Mary (patroness of expectant mothers)

Aloysius Gonzaga, Jesuit (patron of youth)

Barbara (a protectress against lightning)

Augustine, bishop of Hippo (patron of brewers and theologians)

Thomas Aquinas, philosopher and theologian (a patron adopted by schools)

Helen, divorced (patroness of converts and those who struggle with marriage problems)

Agnes, martyr (patroness of victims of rape)

Frances Cabrini (patroness of immigrants and orphans, also adopted by hospitals)

Bernard of Clairvaux, abbot (patron of candle makers and those who have a special love of Mary)

Thomas, the apostle (patron of architects and those who harbor doubts)

Clare of Assisi, foundress of the Poor Clares (patroness of those affiliated with television)

Cecilia (patroness of musicians, organ builders, singers, and poets)

Frances of Rome (patroness of motorists and those with a special devotion to guardian angels)

Francis de Sales, founder of the Order of the Visitation (patron of authors and those with hearing impairments)

Isaac Jogues, Jesuit and martyr (patron of missionaries)

Mary Magdalen (patroness of repentant sinners and prostitutes)

Martha (patroness of cooks, dietitians, servants, maids, and of those whose focus is hospitality)

Peregrine of Auxerre (patron of those who suffer with cancer)

Pope Pius X (patron of those devoted to frequently receiving Communion)

That the angels and the Saints have intercessory **Patron Saints**
power before God on behalf of human needs and
concerns is a basic Catholic belief. At times God has
intervened in human lives through the Saints' intercessions. In Catholic tradition, the Saints are classi-
fied as "patrons" because they are known to help in
varied and specific ways. Churches, dioceses, and
countries usually have their patron Saints as special
protectors and intercessors.

The Fourteen Holy Helpers, for example, were
popular in the Rhineland in the fourteenth century.
Why fourteen and why these Saints have been singled
out are open to conjecture. Although criticized by the
reformers and discouraged by the Council of Trent,
the custom of devotion to the Fourteen Holy Helpers
still endures in certain areas.

The following list associates Saints, some well
known and others obscure, with the concerns for
which they are noted.

Acacius, third-century bishop: patron of those
    who suffer headaches

Barbara, imprisoned in a tower: patroness
    associated with lightning

Blaise, bishop and martyr: patron of those who
    suffer throat diseases

Catherine of Alexandria, martyr: patroness of
    philosophers and debaters

Christopher, known as a "Christ-bearer": patron
    of travelers

Cyricus, martyred deacon: patron of those who
    suffer eye diseases

Denis, a French martyr: patron of those who suffer with rabies and headaches

Erasmus (Elmo), martyr: patron of those who suffer intestinal problems

Eustace, hunter and Roman general: patron protector against fires

George, dragon slayer: patron of those who suffer skin diseases

Giles, eighth-century hermit: patron of those who suffer with epilepsy

Margaret of Antioch: patroness of those facing childbirth

Pantaleon, martyr whose blood liquefies: patron of those who suffer with cancer or tuberculosis

Vitus, Roman martyr: patron of those who suffer with epilepsy

Nominees for Sainthood

The saintly goodness of the individuals mentioned thus far come to us from across the centuries. Yet, many people in our time are likely candidates for sainthood. They include:

Bishop Oscar Romero (1917-1980): Archbishop of El Salvador; slain while preaching for the rights of the poor and oppressed; canonization cause in process

Thomas Merton (1915-1968): Trappist monk and spiritual writer of over fifty books; advocate of tolerance and unity in the midst of pluralistic spiritual views

Pierre Teilhard de Chardin (1881-1955): Jesuit anthropologist with cosmic vision, whose evolutionary theory viewed Christ as the Omega Point toward which all reality tends

Dorothy Day (1897-1980): founder of the Catholic Worker Movement and advocate of social justice, nonviolence, voluntary poverty, and hospitality

Pope John XXIII (1881-1963): a pope of vision and foresight; instrumental in the renewal of the Church; convoked the Second Vatican Council

Papal Saints

Of the 262 popes in the two-thousand-year history of the Church, eighty popes are canonized Saints. Surprisingly, seventy-four of these popes reigned before A.D. 900. Leo IX (1049), Gregory VII Hildebrand (1073), and Celestine (1294) are the three papal Saints of the early Middle Ages.

The fourteenth and fifteenth centuries produced no papal Saints, for it was a time of turmoil and corruption within the Church.

Pope Pius V (1572) is a Saint from the age of the Counter-Reformation. Pius X (1914) is the papal Saint of the twentieth century. Eight popes are "blessed," most of whom reigned between the eleventh and fourteenth centuries.

Pope John Paul II can be called the "pope of Saints." To date, he has canonized 275 Saints in thirty-six ceremonies. This includes three collective canonizations: 103 Korean martyrs, 16 martyrs of Japan, and 117 Vietnamese martyrs. He also conducted the first canonization outside of Rome, in Korea in 1994.

Pope John Paul II has also been prolific in beatifications. He has held 212 individual and eleven collective beatifications, for a total of 622 new "blesseds" (according to the *1996 Catholic Almanac*).

All in the Family

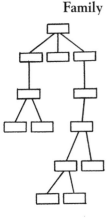

As we review history, we find that sainthood often seems to "run in the family." We find siblings who are Saints, parents and their children who are Saints, spouses who are Saints, grandparents and grandchildren who are Saints.

The following list separates Saints according to their familial relationships:

Sibling Saints: Peter and Andrew (apostles); James and John (apostles); Benedict and Scholastica (known for their monastic way of life); Cyril and Methodius (apostles to Slovakia); Cosmas and Damian (martyred physicians); King Louis of France and Isabella (missionaries and crusaders); Faustinus and Jovita (martyrs); Primus and Felicianus (martyrs); Marcus and Marcillianus (twins, martyrs).

Husband and wife Saints: Mary and Joseph (mother and foster father of Jesus); Elizabeth and Zechariah (parents of John the Baptist); Anne and Joachim (parents of Mary, the mother of Jesus); Priscilla and Aquila (see Acts 18:1, Romans 16:3, and 1 Corinthians 16:19); Crescentia and Modestus (martyrs); Julian and Basilissa (martyrs).

Parent and child Saints: Elizabeth and her son, John the Baptist; Bridget of Sweden and her daughter, Katherine of Sweden; Monica and her son, Augustine of Hippo; Felicity and her seven sons; Clotildis and her son, Gontran.

Other family relationships: Ludmilla and her grandson, Wenceslas; Emiliana and her nephew, Pope Gregory the Great; Pope Felix I and his niece, Thrasilla; Pope Caius and his niece, Susanna; Hedwig of Hungary and her niece, Elizabeth of Hungary; Patrick and his nephew, Mel; Bishop Odo of Canterbury and his nephew, Oswald; Clotilda and her grandson, Cloud.

Saints of royal lineage: Radegundes, queen of Soissons; Bathildis, queen of Paris; Jane of Valois, noble lady in France; Cunegund, empress of Lithuania and Poland; Casimir, king of Poland; Maud, queen of Germany; Stephen, king of Hungary.

Some Saints realized that both masculine and feminine viewpoints can add to one's experience of God. As a result, these Saints formed deep spiritual relationships with members of the opposite sex. Some of the men and women who shared a deep spiritual friendship in the Lord include Jane Frances de Chantal and Francis de Sales; Teresa of Avila and John of the Cross; Margaret Mary Alacoque and Claude de la Colombière; Francis of Assisi and Clare.

A Day for All Saints

We honor all the Saints, including those who have no specific feast, with a solemnity on November 1. It is a feast rich in tradition and antiquity.

In A.D. 609, the Roman Emperor, Phocas, ceded the Pantheon, which had been a pagan temple in honor of all the gods. The edifice was rededicated as a church in honor of Mary and all martyrs on May 13 of that year. In due time, the date was moved to November 1 because that was the day when many pilgrims were in Rome and food was plentiful after the harvest. The date also counteracted the Druid feast of evil spirits, October 31.

Saints' Names

Saints' names carry special meaning. Tradition and history have used the Saints' names for both people and geographical locations.

The naming of children after Saints, for example, began in the early Church, when Christians wanted to keep alive the memory and spirit of those who were being martyred for their faith. Gradually, the custom spread, especially in France and Germany. The Celts and Irish, however, found the practice blasphemous.

Then, the Council of Trent (1545-1563) decreed that all babies baptized *must* take the name of a Saint. If it was doubtful whether the chosen name was a Saint's name, the ordained minister officiating at the baptism inserted the name of a Saint. Today, the Revised Code of Canon Law (3855) declares that the name given at baptism cannot be contrary to Christian values.

San Antonio

Naming a geographic location after a Saint more or less commemorates the location to the memory and patronage of that particular Saint. Names of some American sites that bear Saints' names are Saint Augustine, Florida; San Antonio, Texas; Saint Louis, Missouri; Saint Paul, Minnesota; and Mount Saint Helens, Washington. California is dotted with places with Saints' names: San Bernardino, Santa Clara, San

Clemente, Santa Ana, San Jose, San Rafael, Santa Barbara, San Fernando, San Francisco, Santa Monica, Santa Rosa, and San Diego.

Some folk customs linger. The custom of saying "God bless you" after a sneeze, for example, began with Gregory the Great, who recommended it during a pestilence; it was believed that when one sneezes, the vital signs cease and one is in the grip of the devil.

Saintly Folk Customs

Some Saints live on through customs and practices that were inspired by their lives and example. Some of the more commonly known traditions include:

Blaise (February 3): Blaise, a bishop of Armenia in the fourth century, saved a child from choking on a fish bone. The Church invokes Blaise's protection against throat diseases by blessing throats on his feast day. Two blessed candles are held to one's chin with the blessing: "Through the intercession of Blaise, bishop and martyr, may you be preserved from all ills of the throat, through Christ our Lord."

Valentine (February 14): One reason we send valentines and tokens of love and friendship on February 14 comes from a legend about Valentine, a fourth-century martyr priest who sent to his people notes of encouragement on heart-shaped violet leaves growing outside his prison cell. Today, the custom is a lucrative secular holiday. Greeting card companies and florists are especially happy that this tradition endures.

Patrick (March 17): Because of the large number of persons of Irish descent in the United States, March 17 has evolved into a cultural holiday, with the color green dominating the day. The kindly bishop who brought the faith to Ireland is remembered with parades, food, music, and merriment. In Ireland it is marked primarily as a religious holy day. Patrick is usually pictured with the shamrock because he used it to teach the mystery of the Trinity.

Joseph (March 19): The custom of sharing one's food and inviting persons to a meal on Joseph's feast, March 19, originated among Sicilian Catholics. Blessed bread, pastries, and other food are given to the poor on this feast, usually called Saint Joseph's Table. The swallows also return to San Juan Capistrano mission in California on Saint Joseph's Day.

Swithin (July 15): Although Swithin, Bishop of Winchester in the ninth century, requested that he be buried outdoors, his brother monks decided to reinter his body in the church when he was canonized. When a forty-day rain ensued, however, it was interpreted as a sign of the Saint's disapproval. The custom spread; the weather on Saint Swithin's Day, July 15, is an omen for forty days of good or bad weather.

Christopher (July 25): Though his historical reality is questioned, Christopher is still popular. Legend says that he carried people across a river, and that one day he actually carried the Christ Child. He is known as the patron of travelers. Many drivers still affix a medal or statue of Christopher on the car dashboard for protection from accidents.

Januarius (September 19): Januarius was a fourth-century bishop who was executed under the emperor, Diocletian. Januarius' blood liquefies on his feast, September 19, and other times, which portends blessings for the city of Naples, Italy.

Francis of Assisi (October 4): Francis of Assisi is known for his love of nature and animals. As a result, the tradition of blessing animals on his feast day has become quite popular. Not only Catholics, but animal lovers, humane societies, and veterinarians call on Catholic priests to pray to Francis for the well-being of the animals.

Nicholas (December 6): Bishop Nicholas of Myra, known for his generosity in gift-giving, is the inspiration for Santa Claus. In some countries, people still receive gifts on his feast, December 6. My Austrian grandmother brought this custom with her to this country. Each year on Saint Nicholas Day, a jovial Irish bachelor who lived nearby donned his red suit and canvassed the neighborhood throwing goodies into the houses as families were seated at supper.

Conclusion

This collection of facts, traditions, and customs surrounding Saints is like looking at sanctity through a kaleidoscope. Each Saint is an ideal representation of virtue, but each one mirrors holiness in a unique way. There are Saints for cities and countries, for special causes, for unique prayer styles, and for personality types. Each human need and aspiration has a Saint advocate.

With this panorama, Catholics cannot possibly know or have devotion to each Saint. The panoply of Saints, however, enables us to have models according to our individual needs and tastes.

The gallery of Saints is a precious heritage representing all nations, cultures, ages, and occupations. Not every Saint perfectly mirrors the grandeur of God, but each is a single kaleidoscopic image of the Divine. Put together, the Saints are a grand symphony of virtue and holiness, each playing a part in perfect harmony and producing their unique melody of eternal love.

The Saints are enigmas and mysteries because they exhibit familiarity with the Lord. The Saints portray to us divine presence in the world. Their lives inspire us to greater heights of holiness and deeper areas of intimacy with God. While a work of this scope contains only a sparse overview of the Saints, it would be a worthwhile exercise to read the details of their lives.

Regardless of the era we live in, or what destiny or circumstances of life we face, we all have our share of gifts and graces. We have the lives of these noble souls to speak to us of courage, fidelity, and faith.

When we scan the lives of the Saints, we undoubtedly find a human being with whom we can relate. We find one who has the exact situations in life that we face. By finding out how that Saint overcame those same situations, we are inspired and edified. By considering and meditating on the Saints, we move beyond our pettiness and are able to put things in perspective. Quiet reflection on how a Saint handled a difficult situation helps us see things in a different light. It helps us rearrange our own life in a way that allows us to live fulfilled and meaningfully on that plane we call "spirituality," a closeness and affinity with God.

The Saints are with us, and the Church has thanked God in every age for that gift of their presence and example. We are grateful for a Church that will continue to produce hearty souls and eminent Saints. The promise of the Lord, "I am with you always" (Matthew 28:20), is dutifully fulfilled in the Saints.

About the Author

Sister Charlene Altemose, MSC is a Missionary Sister of the Most Sacred Heart (Reading, Pennsylvania) with degrees in education, theology, and journalism. Her ministries have included teaching college the-  ology, writing newspaper columns and articles, directing parish adult education, and being active in interfaith activities and the Council of Churches.

Sister Charlene was awarded a Fullbright scholarship to India and a Christian Leadership grant to Israel. As a result of her scholarship excellence, she was invited to be a presenter at the 1993 Council for a Parliament of World Religions.

Author of Liguori's popular *What You Should Know About…*series (*What You Should Know About the Mass*; *What You Should Know About the Catechism of the Catholic Church*; *What You Should Know About the Sacraments*; *What You Should Know About Angels*), Sister Charlene is a popular speaker at workshops, retreats, and in-service or adult education programs.